Cindy's Cellar

by Sydnie Meltzer Kleinhenz
illustrated by Colin Thompson

Harcourt

Orlando Boston Dallas Chicago San Diego

Visit *The Learning Site!*

www.harcourtschool.com

Cindy always did like surprises. Once she found a special door in her cellar.

Cindy saw a place that was almost too pretty to look at. She raced up the hill.

She heard the sound of a dance. A prince glanced at her.

The prince even asked her to dance. Cindy does like to dance.

They danced and pranced. They whirled around with happy faces.

Cindy stopped and said,
"My feet are worn out."
The prince got her a seat.

Then he said he would get parts so she could replace her feet.

He said, "Have some nuts."
Cindy looked twice. What
kind of place is this?

The prince gave Cindy a necklace. He said, "You can be a robot princess."

Cindy didn't know what to say.

Cindy raced back to her cellar. She almost always likes surprises!